EDGE
BOOKS

SPORTS RIVALRIES

OUTRAGEOUS

HOCKEY
RIVALRIES

BY HANS HETRICK

CONSULTANT: CRAIG R. COENEN, PROFESSOR OF HISTORY, MERCER COUNTY COMMUNITY COLLEGE,
WEST WINDSOR, NEW JERSEY

CAPSTONE PRESS
a capstone imprint

Edge Books are published by Capstone Press,
1710 Roe Crest Drive, North Mankato, Minnesota 56003
www.capstonepub.com

Library of Congress Cataloging-in-Publication Data
Cataloging-in-publication information is on file with the Library of Congress.
ISBN 978-1-4914-2027-0 (library binding)
ISBN 978-1-4914-2198-7 (eBook PDF)

Editorial Credits
Angie Kaelberer and Alesha Sullivan, editors; Ted Williams, designer;
Eric Gohl, media researcher; Tori Abraham, production specialist

Photo Credits
AP Photo: Cal Sports Media, cover (bottom), The Canadian Press/Paul Chiasson,
cover (top); CriaImages.com: Jay Robert Nash Collection, 6–7; Getty Images:
Allsport/Ted Mathias, 22–23, Bruce Bennett Studios, 16, NHLI/Denis Brodeur, 9;
Newscom: ABACAUSA.COM/Chuck Myers, 24–25, Cal Sport Media/Mike Wulf,
1, Icon SMI/Ian Harding, 12–13, 14–15, Icon SMI/John Cordes, 18–19, Icon SMI/
Michael Tureski, 5, 26–27, Icon SMI/Tony Ding, 20–21, KRT/Jim Gehrz, 29, UPI Photo
Service/Brian Gadbery, 10, ZUMA Press/Frank Lennon, 12 (inset)

Design Elements
Shutterstock

Printed in the United States of America in Stevens Point, Wisconsin
092014   008479WZS15

Table of Contents

A GAME OF INTENSITY

Few sports can match the intensity of pro hockey. It's played at lightning speeds. A National Hockey League (NHL) hockey puck is the fastest-moving object in professional team sports. Most **slap shots** clock in at more than 100 miles (161 kilometers) per hour. Only **goalies** with the most amazing reflexes and acrobatics can stop them. The other players are fast too. They can reach speeds of nearly 30 miles (48 km) per hour on their skates. With all of that speed, the collisions are tremendous. That's one reason some hockey players are missing a few teeth.

NHL fans share the intensity of the game. The only thing separating the players and the fans is a thin sheet of shatter-resistant glass above the **boards**. Fans can hear every **hockey stop**, every puck that hits the goalie's pads, and every slap shot. Players can hear the fans pounding on the glass. They can hear their insults and cheers. Because they share so much, NHL players and the fans have a strong bond.

The NHL has produced many fierce rivalries. The fans created some of these rivalries. Others started with the players. But it doesn't matter how a rivalry began. The fans and players build the NHL's greatest rivalries together.

The Montreal Canadiens and the Boston Bruins fight for a loose puck during the Eastern Conference Quarterfinals game in 2011.

slap shot—the fastest and most forceful shot in hockey

goalie—a player who guards the goal and tries to prevent the opponent's shots from going into the net

boards—the wall sections around a hockey rink

hockey stop—a method of stopping while skating; the player stops abruptly by digging the skate edges into the ice

ORIGINAL SIX

The NHL was organized in 1917. In the early years, a lot of teams came and went. By 1942 only six teams remained. For 25 years these six teams battled for the Stanley Cup. Every regular-season game was a rivalry game. Every playoff series was a struggle. The six teams are now known as the "Original Six."

ORIGINAL SIX TEAMS

Boston Bruins
Chicago Black Hawks
Detroit Red Wings
Montreal Canadiens
New York Rangers
Toronto Maple Leafs

Two of the Original Six teams, the Rangers and Maple Leafs, battle in the 1960s.

NHL DIVISIONS

NHL teams belong to a conference and a division. There are two conferences, the Western and Eastern. Each conference has two divisions. During playoffs, each division champion plays the other in the conference. Then each conference champion plays for the Stanley Cup.

EASTERN CONFERENCE

Atlantic Division
Boston Bruins
Buffalo Sabres
Detroit Red Wings
Florida Panthers
Montreal Canadiens
Ottawa Senators
Tampa Bay Lightning
Toronto Maple Leafs

Metropolitan Division
Carolina Hurricanes
Columbus Blue Jackets
New Jersey Devils
New York Islanders
New York Rangers
Philadelphia Flyers
Pittsburgh Penguins
Washington Capitals

WESTERN CONFERENCE

Central Division
Chicago Blackhawks
Colorado Avalanche
Dallas Stars
Minnesota Wild
Nashville Predators
St. Louis Blues
Winnipeg Jets

Pacific Division
Anaheim Ducks
Calgary Flames
Edmonton Oilers
Los Angeles Kings
Phoenix Coyotes
San Jose Sharks
Vancouver Canucks

MAPLE LEAFS
VS.
CANADIENS

The Toronto and Montreal rivalry is as old as the NHL. The Maple Leafs and Canadiens are the only two surviving members from the NHL's first season. Both teams have been successful, and no two teams have claimed more Stanley Cups.

The teams represent two very different parts of Canada. Toronto is the largest English-speaking city in Canada. Montreal is the largest French-speaking city in Canada. The rivalry was at its fiercest during the NHL's Original Six era. The Maple Leafs and Canadiens were the only Canadian teams in the league. Canadian fans either cheered for the Maple Leafs or the Canadiens.

In the 1960s the rivalry reached epic levels. These teams won nine Stanley Cups—four for the Leafs and five for the Canadiens. Surprisingly they faced off just twice in the Finals during that time. Montreal won in 1960, and Toronto won in 1967.

Montreal holds the top bragging rights in the rivalry. The Canadiens have won an amazing 23 Stanley Cups while the Maple Leafs have won 13. But in the five Cup Finals where they've faced each other, the Maple Leafs own a three-to-two advantage. That fact stings Canadiens fans enough to keep this rivalry flaming.

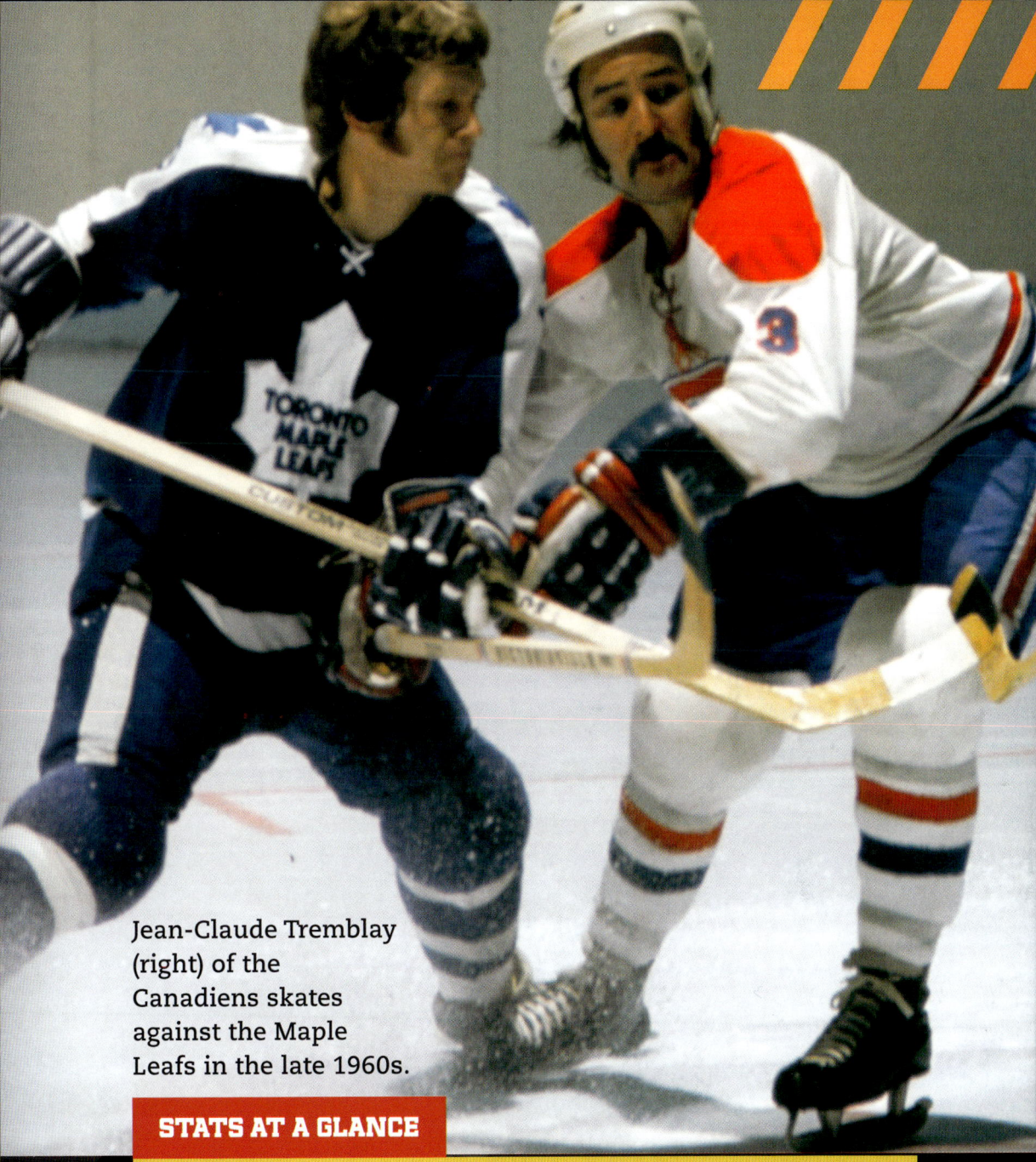

Jean-Claude Tremblay (right) of the Canadiens skates against the Maple Leafs in the late 1960s.

STATS AT A GLANCE

MAPLE LEAFS

1st NHL Season: 1917
Stanley Cups: 13
Stanley Cup Appearances: 21
Star Players: Frank Mahovlich, Turk Broda, Mats Sundin, Phil Kessel

CANADIENS

1st NHL Season: 1917
Stanley Cups: 23
Stanley Cup Appearances: 32
Star Players: Maurice "Rocket" Richard, Guy Lafleur, Ken Dryden, Tomáš Plekanec

AVALANCHE
VS.
RED WINGS

Steve Yzerman (19) of the Red Wings fires a shot at the net in a 1996 match against the Avalanche.

The Red Wings and Avalanche rivalry didn't last long. But it might be the fiercest in NHL history. The five playoff series where the Red Wings and Avalanche faced off between 1996 and 2002 are now legendary. The hockey was first class. Both teams were loaded with Hall of Fame superstars.

The rivalry turned mean during the 1996 Western Conference Finals. In game six Colorado's Claude Lemieux **checked** Detroit's Kris Draper face-first into the boards. Draper's jaw, nose, and cheekbone were broken, and he also had a concussion. The Red Wings were furious with Lemieux and the rest of his team. The Avalanche won the series. Then they **swept** the Florida Panthers to win the Stanley Cup.

But the Red Wings fought back the next season at a home game at Joe Louis Arena in Detroit. Nine fights broke out between the Avalanche and the Red Wings. One fight near the end of the first **period** included every player on the ice, including the goalies, Patrick Roy and Mike Vernon. Fans called that night "the Brawl in Hockeytown" and "Fight Night at the Joe." The Red Wings won the game 6–5 in overtime. The teams met again in the Western Conference Finals. This time the Red Wings won the series. Then they swept the Philadelphia Flyers to win the Stanley Cup.

During their seven-year rivalry, the Red Wings won three Stanley Cups. The Avalanche won two. The rivalry was so strong that some of the players are still bitter.

check—to slam into another player

sweep—to win all the games in a series

period—a session of play; hockey games have three 20-minute periods

OILERS VS. FLAMES

The rivalry between the Edmonton Oilers and the Calgary Flames runs deep and goes beyond hockey. Edmonton and Calgary were rivals long before the NHL arrived. They are the two largest cities in the Canadian province of Alberta. For more than 100 years, their residents have argued over everything: politics, business, and especially hockey. When the Oilers and Flames face off, a century's worth of disagreements is on display.

In 1979 Edmonton received an NHL team. The next year the Atlanta Flames moved to Calgary. It was an instant rivalry, and the stakes became big very quickly. Both teams qualified for the playoffs in their first year. Within a few years, they were dominating their conference. Between 1983 and 1990, either the Flames or the Oilers represented their conference in the Stanley Cup Finals. But it was the Oilers that captured most of the glory.

Edmonton's star Wayne Gretzky in action in 1981

Oilers right wing Ryan Jones chases the puck as Flames goalie Joey McDonald pokes it away from a pile-up during a 2013 showdown.

STATS AT A GLANCE

OILERS

1st NHL Season: 1979

Stanley Cups: 5

Stanley Cup Appearances: 7

Star Players: Wayne Gretzky, Mark Messier, Paul Coffey, Aleš Hemský

FLAMES

1st NHL Season: 1972 (moved to Calgary in 1980, previously Atlanta Flames)

Stanley Cups: 1

Stanley Cup Appearances: 3

Star Players: Theoren Fleury, Mike Vernon, Al MacInnis, Mark Giordano

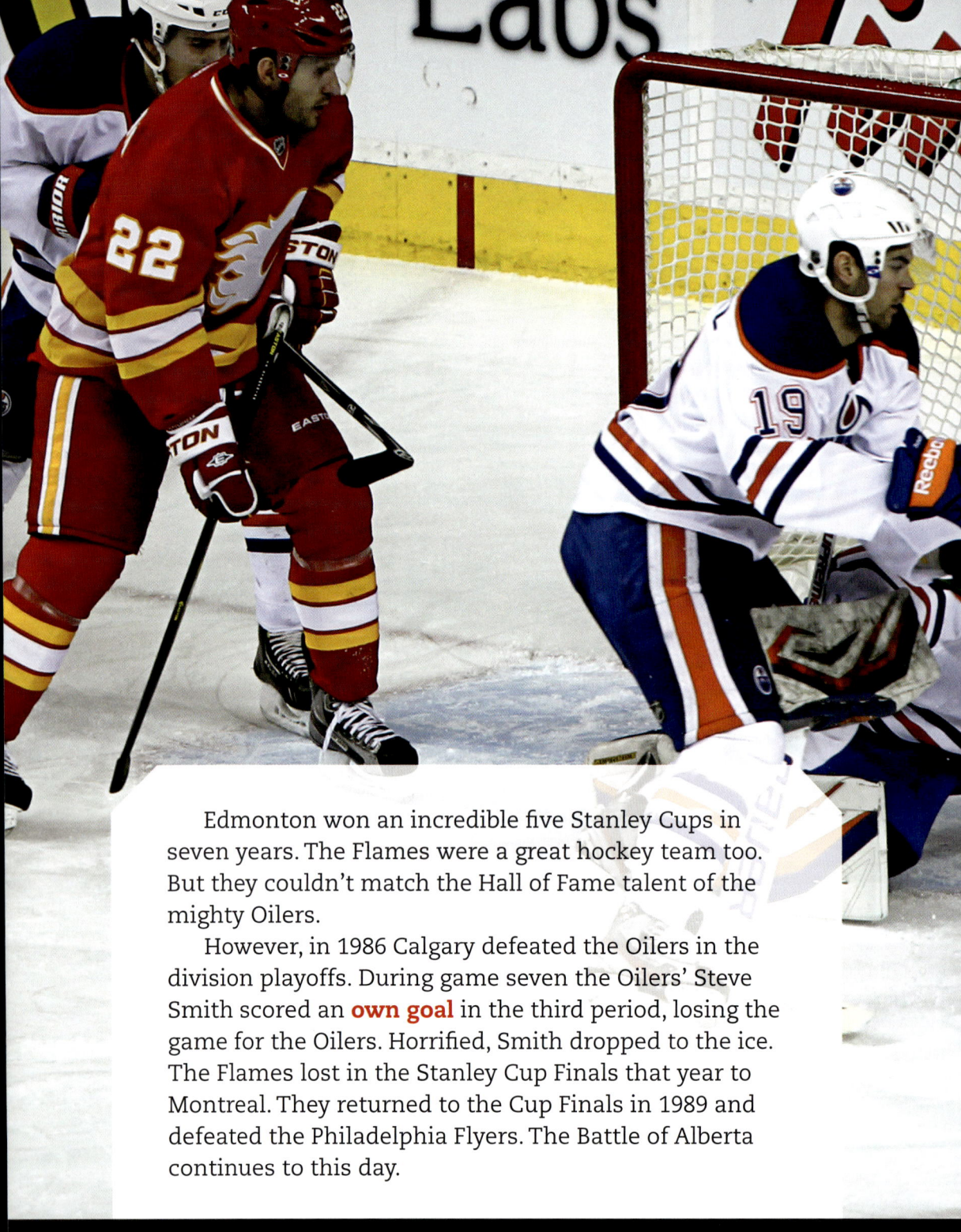

Edmonton won an incredible five Stanley Cups in seven years. The Flames were a great hockey team too. But they couldn't match the Hall of Fame talent of the mighty Oilers.

However, in 1986 Calgary defeated the Oilers in the division playoffs. During game seven the Oilers' Steve Smith scored an **own goal** in the third period, losing the game for the Oilers. Horrified, Smith dropped to the ice. The Flames lost in the Stanley Cup Finals that year to Montreal. They returned to the Cup Finals in 1989 and defeated the Philadelphia Flyers. The Battle of Alberta continues to this day.

own goal—a puck that is shot into a team's own net, scoring a goal for the other team

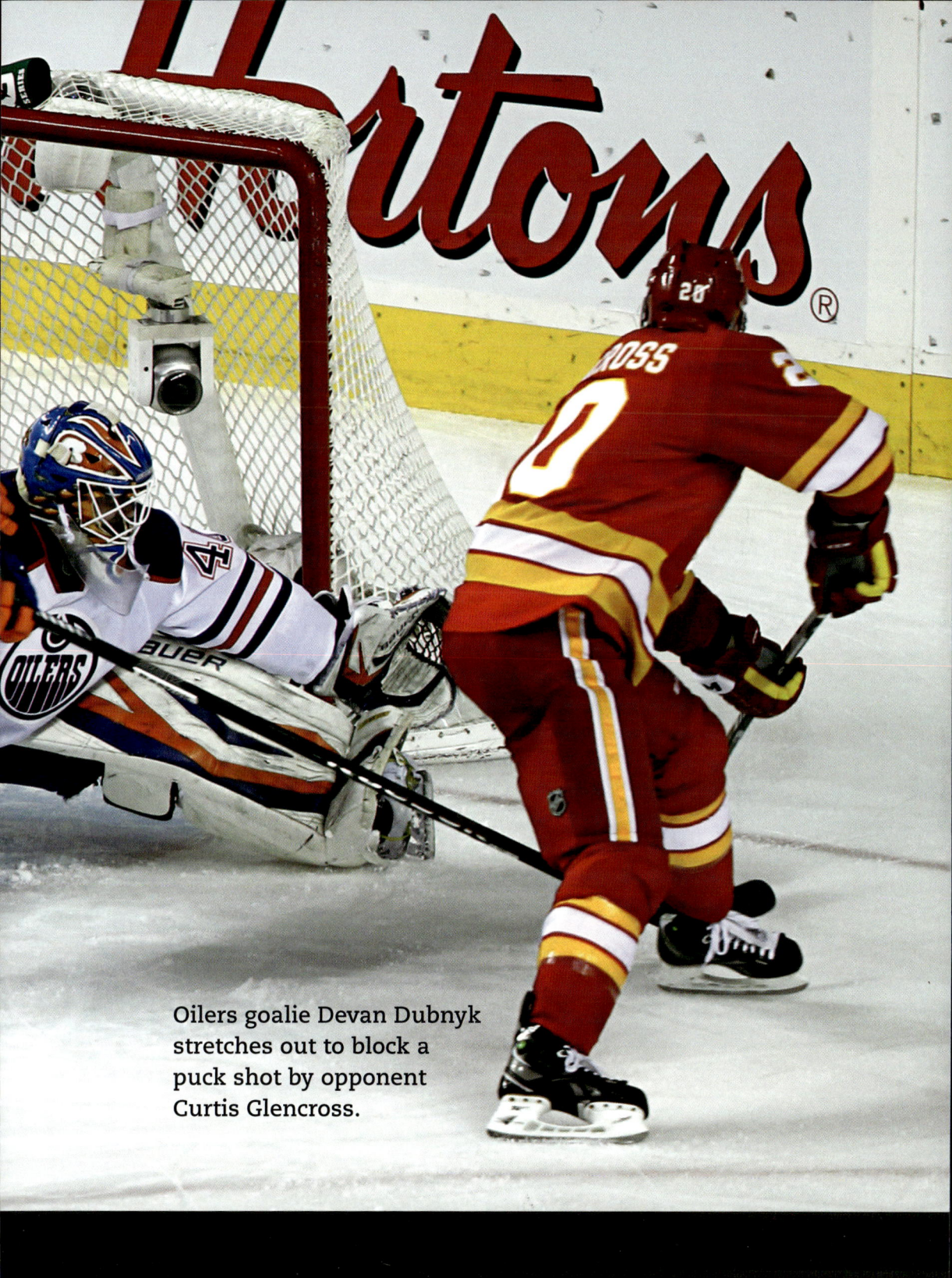

Oilers goalie Devan Dubnyk stretches out to block a puck shot by opponent Curtis Glencross.

RANGERS VS. ISLANDERS

No chant has tortured a hockey team more than "1940." The New York Rangers won the Stanley Cup in 1940. It took them 54 years to win another. Islanders fans loved to remind the Rangers of their long championship drought. Every time the teams faced off, chants of "1940" filled the stadium. And it made the Rangers fans and players furious.

Islanders fans had every right to chant "1940." The Islanders joined the NHL in 1972. Between 1980 and 1983, they won four straight Stanley Cups. After just 11 years, the Islanders had more Stanley Cups than the Rangers. The Rangers were an Original Six team. They had been in the NHL since 1926 but had won just three Stanley Cups.

The Rangers finally won their fourth Stanley Cup in 1994 by defeating the Vancouver Canucks. It was more than a championship to the Rangers. It killed the dreaded "1940" chant forever.

STATS AT A GLANCE

RANGERS
1st NHL Season: 1926
Stanley Cups: 4
Stanley Cup Appearances: 11
Star Players: Brad Park, Brian Leetch, Henrik Lundqvist

ISLANDERS
1st NHL Season: 1972
Stanley Cups: 4
Stanley Cup Appearances: 5
Star Players: Mike Bossy, Denis Potvin, John Tavares

A referee attempts to split up a brawl between the Rangers and Islanders in the 1980s.

THE COMEBACK OF ALL COMEBACKS

The Islanders made history in the 1975 Stanley Cup Quarterfinals. They lost the first three games to the Pittsburgh Penguins. The Islanders fought back. They won the next four games to win the series. Only four other North American pro sports teams have won a seven-game series after losing their first three games. They are the Toronto Maple Leafs, the Philadelphia Flyers, and the Los Angeles Kings, as well as Major League Baseball's Boston Red Sox.

The story of the Kings and the Ducks couldn't have been written anywhere but in Hollywood. A celebrity and movie helped transform southern California into a hockey hot spot. In 1988 star center Wayne Gretzky left the Edmonton Oilers to play for the Kings. Los Angeles has been a great NHL city ever since. The Walt Disney Corporation founded the Mighty Ducks of Anaheim in 1993. *The Mighty Ducks* was a Disney movie about a hockey team of misfit kids. The Ducks were popular their first season and have since built a loyal fan base. In 2005 Disney sold the team, and the name was shortened to the Ducks.

In 2014 the Kings had a tough road to the Stanley Cup. They beat the San Jose Sharks four games to three to get into the Western Conference Semifinals. There they met their rivals, the Ducks. The Kings again had to go seven games before defeating the Ducks. In the Finals they faced the Blackhawks and again the series went seven games before the Kings took the title. In the Stanley Cup the Kings met up with the New York Rangers. That time it only took them five games to win the series and the Cup.

Over the years the two teams have battled many times. As of 2014 the teams are evenly matched, with each winning 53 games and 11 ending in a tie. But the Kings have two Stanley Cups to the Ducks' one.

Ducks right wing Tim Jackman is airborne over Kings goalie Jonathan Quick during a 2014 battle.

OUTDOOR HOCKEY, CALIFORNIA STYLE

On January 25, 2014, the Kings and the Ducks faced off in NHL's Stadium Series. It was the first outdoor NHL game ever in southern California.

That night 54,099 hockey-crazed fans sold out Dodger Stadium. The 63-degree-Fahrenheit (17-degree-Celsius) temperature left the ice soft, but the players managed to skate. The Ducks won the game 3–0, and Californians proved their passion for hockey.

STATS AT A GLANCE

KINGS

1st NHL Season: 1967
Stanley Cups: 2
Stanley Cup Appearances: 3
Star Players: Wayne Gretzky, Luc Robataille, Anže Kopitar, Jonathan Quick

DUCKS

1st NHL Season: 1993
Stanley Cups: 1
Stanley Cup Appearances: 2
Star Players: Teemu Salänne, Ryan Getzlaf, Corey Perry

BLACKHAWKS
VS.
RED WINGS

The Blackhawks and Red Wings rivalry has a rich history. The teams have faced off in more regular season games than any other two NHL teams.

Detroit dominated the rivalry in the 1940s and 1950s. The Red Wings were led by Gordie Howe, Sid Abel, and Ted Lindsay. The trio produced an incredible number of goals, earning them the nickname "The Production Line." In the 1950 NHL season, the three players finished first, second, and third in scoring. Lindsay led the trio that year with 78 **points**. Abel scored 69 points, and Howe had 68. No **first line** has come close to repeating their feat. But the Blackhawks eventually caught up with the Red Wings. Hall of Fame players, including Bobby Hull and Stan Mikita, helped the Blackhawks rise to the top. In 1961 they defeated the Red Wings in a six-game Stanley Cup series.

In 2013 Chicago and Detroit added another amazing chapter to their rivalry. In the Western Conference Semifinals, the Red Wings jumped to 3–1 series lead. The Blackhawks stormed back to win the next three games, the series, and also the Stanley Cup. It was the last time the teams would face each other in division or conference playoffs. Soon after, Detroit moved to the Atlantic division of the Eastern Conference.

point—a hockey statistic; a goal or an assist is equal to one point

first line—the best forward line on a hockey team; a forward line is a group of three offensive players—a center, a left wing, and a right wing

Red Wings goalie Jimmy Howard defends the puck against Blackhawks forward Marcus Krueger in game six of the Western Conference Semifinals in 2013.

STATS AT A GLANCE

BLACKHAWKS
1st NHL Season: 1926
Stanley Cups: 5
Stanley Cup Appearances: 12
Star Players: Bobby Hull, Chris Chelios, Patrick Kane, Jonathan Toews

RED WINGS
1st NHL Season: 1926
Stanley Cups: 11
Stanley Cup Appearances: 24
Star Players: Gordie Howe, Terry Sawchuk, Steve Yzerman, Pavel Datsyuk

FLYERS VS. PENGUINS

The Penguins and Flyers both are from Pennsylvania, but they aren't friendly neighbors. Penguins fans think the Flyers are bullies. Flyers fans think the Penguins are stuck-up. Flyers fans have a special dislike for Penguins star Sidney Crosby. Crosby quickly learned that the Penguins and Flyers rivalry was no joke. He lost his front teeth in 2005. It was during one of his first games in Philadelphia after a check from Flyers' Derian Hatcher. Hatcher didn't receive a penalty, but Crosby did after he complained to the officials.

The Battle for Pennsylvania might be the craziest rivalry in the NHL. One of the wildest episodes happened during a 1989 playoff game. The Penguins' Rob Brown scored to put his team ahead 9–2. Brown celebrated his goal with a windmill fist pump. Flyers' goalie Ron Hextall didn't like Brown's celebration during the lopsided game. Hextall chased Brown around the rink, swinging his goalie stick in the air.

STATS AT A GLANCE

FLYERS

1st NHL Season: 1967
Stanley Cups: 2
Stanley Cup Appearances: 8
Star Players: Bobby Clarke, Eric Lindros, Claude Giroux

PENGUINS

1st NHL Season: 1967
Stanley Cups: 3
Stanley Cup Appearances: 4
Star Players: Mario Lemieux, Jaromír Jágr, Evgeni Malkin, Sidney Crosby

Eddie Olczyk falls into Flyers left wing John LeClair during a Penguins 5–3 loss to the Flyers in 1997.

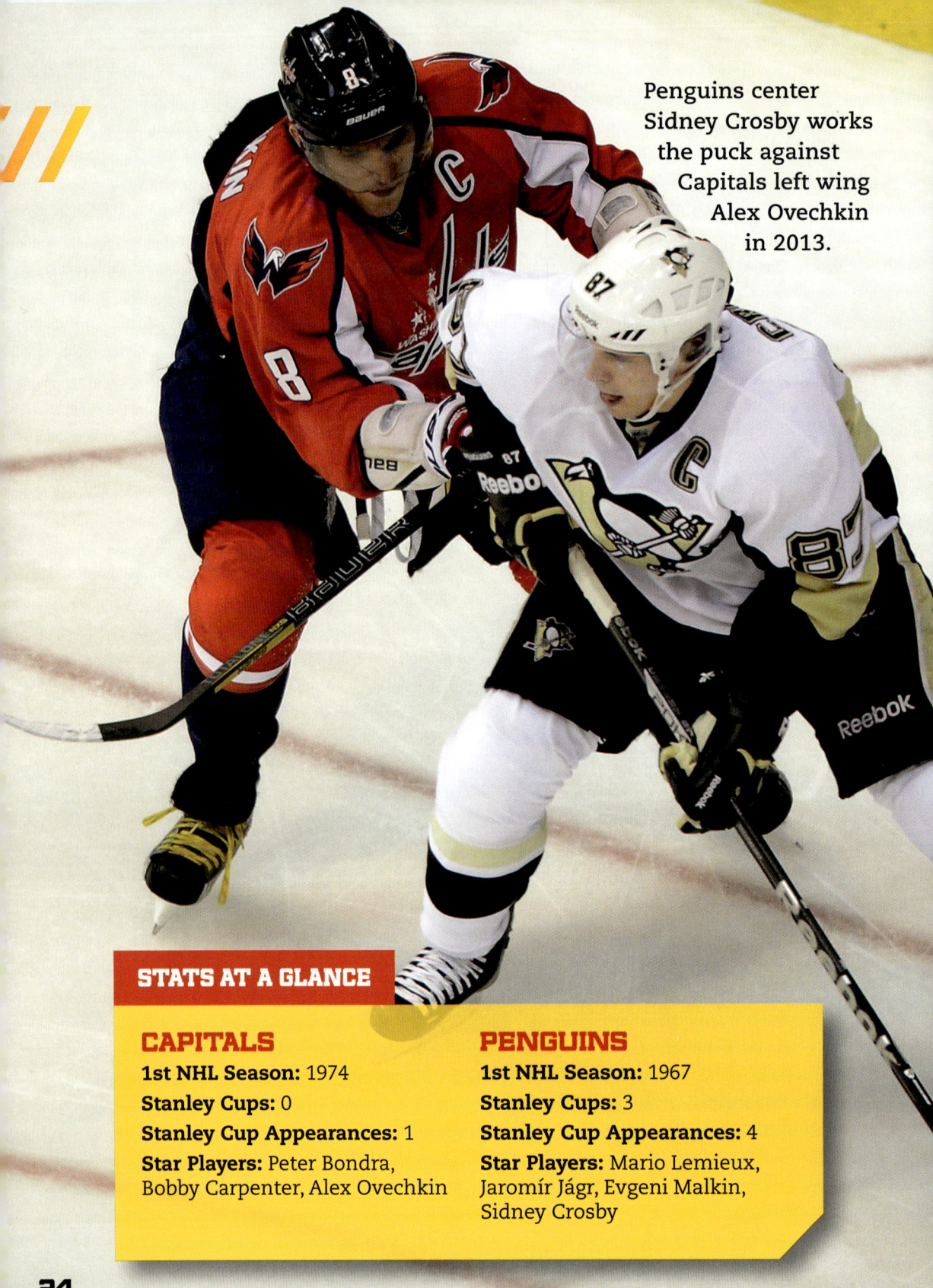

Penguins center Sidney Crosby works the puck against Capitals left wing Alex Ovechkin in 2013.

STATS AT A GLANCE

CAPITALS
1st NHL Season: 1974
Stanley Cups: 0
Stanley Cup Appearances: 1
Star Players: Peter Bondra, Bobby Carpenter, Alex Ovechkin

PENGUINS
1st NHL Season: 1967
Stanley Cups: 3
Stanley Cup Appearances: 4
Star Players: Mario Lemieux, Jaromír Jágr, Evgeni Malkin, Sidney Crosby

CAPITALS VS. PENGUINS

In the 1990s the Washington Capitals had a great hockey team. Unfortunately for them, they were in the same conference as the Pittsburgh Penguins. The Penguins had Mario Lemieux, one of the greatest hockey players of the decade. Between 1991 and 1996, the Capitals and Penguins faced off in five playoff series. The Capitals won just one. The Capitals have always played well against the Penguins. But that only added to their frustration. In 1992 and 1995, the Capitals held a 3–1 series lead. During both years the Penguins won the series with three straight victories.

The Capitals and Penguins rivalry has been renewed in recent years by two superstars. The Penguins' Sidney Crosby and the Capitals' Alexander Ovechkin have very different styles. The low-key Crosby plays hockey with speed and amazing skill. Ovechkin is a fireball. He loves to deliver a hit, and he loves to celebrate goals even more. In 2009 the two superstars met in the Eastern Conference Semifinals. The series went seven games, with five decided by just one goal. Pittsburgh ended up winning the series and went on to win the Stanley Cup.

BRUINS VS. CANADIENS

The Bruins and Canadiens have one of the greatest rivalries in sports. It has a longer history than the Los Angeles Lakers and Boston Celtics' basketball rivalry. It has decided more championships than the Chicago Bears and Green Bay Packers' football rivalry. It has created drama at the level of the Boston Red Sox and New York Yankees' baseball rivalry.

The Boston Bruins and Montreal Canadiens have faced off more than 800 times. They have played 34 playoff series. Nine of those series have gone to seven games, which is an NHL record. The Canadiens have dominated the rivalry, winning 25 of the series.

The rivalry was never more intense than in game seven of the 1979 Semifinals. The Bruins were penalized for having too many players on the ice with just more than two minutes left in the game. During the **power play**, the Canadiens' Guy Lafleur tied the game. The Canadiens won the game in overtime. They went on to win one of their 23 Stanley Cups.

Recently the rivalry has turned in the Bruins' favor. In the 2011 Eastern Conference Quarterfinals, the Bruins defeated the Canadiens in overtime of game seven. They went on to win one of their six Stanley Cups. In 2014 the teams met again in the Conference Semifinals. This time the Canadiens won the series in seven games. But they fell to the New York Rangers in the Finals.

power play—a period of time after one team receives a penalty, resulting in one or more of the team's players leaving the ice

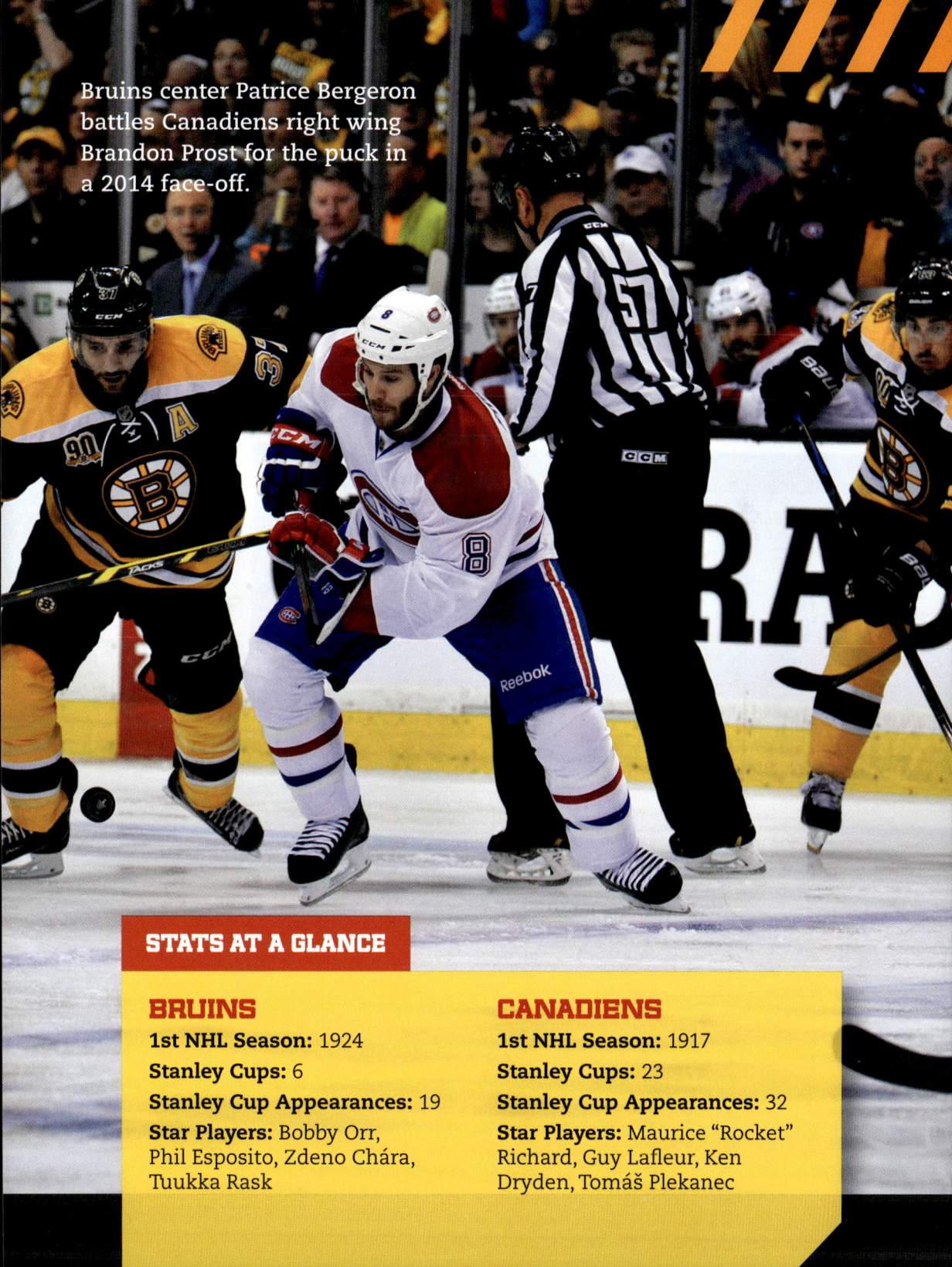

Bruins center Patrice Bergeron battles Canadiens right wing Brandon Prost for the puck in a 2014 face-off.

STATS AT A GLANCE

BRUINS
1st NHL Season: 1924
Stanley Cups: 6
Stanley Cup Appearances: 19
Star Players: Bobby Orr, Phil Esposito, Zdeno Chára, Tuukka Rask

CANADIENS
1st NHL Season: 1917
Stanley Cups: 23
Stanley Cup Appearances: 32
Star Players: Maurice "Rocket" Richard, Guy Lafleur, Ken Dryden, Tomáš Plekanec

WILD
VS.
CANUCKS

The Minnesota Wild joined the NHL in 2000. Just two years into their existence, the Wild had a full-blown rivalry with the Canucks. The two teams could hardly finish a game without a fight or an outburst.

The rivalry really heated up in the 2003 Western Conference Semifinals. During the series the Canucks' Todd Bertuzzi became the biggest villain in Minnesota. The Canucks raced out to a 3–1 series lead. Bertuzzi was confident the Canucks would win game five. He told a group of Wild fans not to bother buying tickets for game six. The Wild won game five and game six, but Bertuzzi wasn't finished. In game seven the Canucks built a 2–0 lead. Bertuzzi taunted the Wild players on the bench. He told them to get out their golf clubs. He meant that the Wild were finished for the season and would have time to play golf. But the Wild came back to win the game 4–2 and the series.

PASSION FOR THE GAME

Hockey may be the world's most action-packed and intense sport. Its players and fans share a passion and a bond like no other. The rivalries this bond creates will keep pro hockey an exciting sport for seasons to come.

The Wild and the Canucks compete for a victory during game seven of the Stanley Cup playoffs in 2003.

STATS AT A GLANCE

WILD

1st NHL Season: 2000

Stanley Cups: 0

Stanley Cup Appearances: 0

Star Players: Marián Gáborík, Mikko Koivu, Zach Parise, Ryan Suter

CANUCKS

1st NHL Season: 1970

Stanley Cups: 0

Stanley Cup Appearances: 3

Star Players: Pavel Bure, Stan Smyl, Daniel Sedin, Henrik Sedin

Glossary

boards (BORDZ)—the wall sections around a hockey rink

check (CHEK)—to slam into another player; most checks don't result in penalties

face-off (FAYSS-awf)—when a player from each team battles for possession of the puck to start or restart play

first line (FURST LINE)—the best forward line on a hockey team; a forward line is a group of three offensive players—a center, a left wing, and a right wing

goalie (GOH-lee)—a player who guards the goal and tries to prevent the opponent's shots from going into the net

hockey stop (HOK-ee STOP)—a method of stopping while skating; the player stops abruptly by digging the skate edges into the ice

own goal (OHN GOHL)—a puck that is shot into a team's own net, scoring a goal for the other team

period (PIHR-ee-uhd)—a session of play; hockey games have three 20-minute periods

point (POINT)—a hockey statistic; a goal or an assist is equal to one point

power play (POU-uhr PLAY)—a period of time after one team receives a penalty, resulting in one or more of the team's players leaving the ice, giving the opposing team an advantage

slap shot (SLAP SHOT)—the fastest and most forceful shot in hockey; a player raises his or her stick and slaps the puck hard toward the goal, putting his or her full body power behind it

sweep (SWEEP)—to win all the games in a series

Read More

Frederick, Shane. *Hockey Legends in the Making.* Legends in the Making. North Mankato, Minn.: Capstone Press, 2014.

Gitlin, Martin. *The Stanley Cup: All about Pro Hockey's Biggest Event.* Winner Takes All. North Mankato, Minn.: Capstone Press, 2013.

Hawkins, Jeff. *Playing Pro Hockey.* Playing Pro Sports. Minneapolis: Lerner Publications Company, 2015.

Internet Sites

FactHound offers a safe, fun way to find Internet sites related to this book. All of the sites on FactHound have been researched by our staff.

Here's all you do:

Visit *www.facthound.com*

Type in this code: 9781491420270

Super-cool stuff!

Check out projects, games and lots more at
www.capstonekids.com

Index